The Old Girls' Book of Dreams

How to Make Your Wishes Come True
Day by Day and Night by Night

Cal Garrison

Red Wheel
Boston, MA / York Beach, ME

First published in 2003 by
Red Wheel/Weiser, LLC
York Beach, ME
With offices at:
368 Congress Street
Boston, MA 02210
www.redwheelweiser.com

Library of Congress Cataloging-in-Publication Data

Garrison, Cal.
   The old girls' book of dreams : how to make your wishes come true day
by day and night by night / Cal Garrison.
      p. cm.
   ISBN 1-59003-062-1
   1. Astrology. 2. Witchcraft. 3. Women--Miscellanea. I. Title.
   BF1729.W64G37 2003
   133.4'3--dc21

                              2003007753

Typeset in Kennerly

Printed in Canada

TCP

10 09 08 07 06 05 04 03
 8 7 6 5 4 3 2 1

This book is for my teacher, Drunvalo Melchizedek,
with love and gratitude for everything
he has taught me and for all the incredible
work he is doing to bring light to the planet.

CONTENTS

DREAMING UP

I am here to remind you to remember how to dream.

When we were kids, we were allowed to wish for things we wanted and hold the dream that we could have them, that our wishes could come true. As we got older, we were instructed by our elders to stop being so childish, and to grow up. What we did as kids *wasn't* childish. If we can reclaim the gift of dreams, we will have the power to change everything–not just in our own lives, but on the planet as well.

There are tons of self-help books and books on affirmations that talk about this stuff. With everything that's already out there, why in God's name am I writing a book about dreams? I am clear enough about my own uniqueness to know for sure that I didn't come to this planet to be redundant! What's already out there is fine, but I have something new to add, so listen closely: Whatever you dream about needs to be dreamt from the *heart,* not the mind. We live in a polarized reality; the mind is polarized like everything else. There's the left brain and the right brain, and the mind sees everything as bad or good, black or white, yin or yang. Whenever you create or conjure up a dream in your mind, something of equal but opposite force will come into being along with whatever you're trying to manifest. It's just the way things are here in our 3D universe.

The heart, on the other hand, is a place of Unity and Unconditional Love. When you craft your dreams in the heart space, they come out exactly as you want them to, without any opposing influence. The way to enter the heart space is very simple; I explain how to do this a little later. This Book of Dreams will help you to write down your dreams *from your heart* and come up with ways you can make them come true.

If it's easier for you to think of this as a journal, be my guest. Whatever's going on with you on any given day will be up or down, bad or good, and there is tremendous value in finding space and time to connect with what you're feeling and thinking. Those issues either support or detract from whatever your real dreams might be and ironing them out is an essential part of the dream process.

So, what are dreams? When we're asleep we dream, and one-third of our life is spent in the dreamtime. Most of us have no clue about how important this aspect of our everyday experience is, but the truth is our sleeping dreams are just as important as what we do when we're awake. There is a continuous flow between the dream state and the waking state, and if you can connect with that flow you'll have a much deeper understanding of what you're here for. Ultimately you'll have the capacity to change aspects of your life and yourself that we've all been taught to believe we have absolutely no control over.

Besides the dreaming we do when we're asleep, there's another kind of dreaming: what we do when we conjure up in our minds things that we want and wish for. I am writing this book to help you see that the power of our dreams is probably stronger than any other force on the planet.

In the '40s and '50s, our parents had just come out of World War II, and the paradigm in place at that time was very different than the one we have now. God bless our parents! If they hadn't been so hell-bent on keeping the world safe for democracy none of us would have the freedom to ponder the deeper meaning of life. Through the next three decades, the illusion of safety our parents created got blown to bits, but this allowed us to explore ourselves and our relationship to the world in ways that very few of our parents had the time or luxury even to consider. So here we are, products of an era where things were pretty black and white. It's clear to me, and probably to you, that in spite of our conditioning nothing is really that simple. Reality isn't a universally agreed-upon thing. What's real for anyone is whatever they're able to dream. What a wonderful paradox! After years of being told that we need to stop dreaming and grow up, we come to see that whatever we can allow ourselves to "dream up" is what becomes real for us.

There's a certain kind of wisdom and understanding that only comes with age. Our connection to our psychic abilities—our Sixth Sense—and our ability to tap into them actually strengthens as we become women of a certain age, or Crones. And the older you get, the more you have to come to terms with your Shadow Self.

The Shadow Self is the part of our selves that we repress or don't want to come to terms with because it's too painful or too frightening. The part of you that wants to kill your boyfriend's lover, for instance, is as alive as the part of you that wants to forgive her. But before you can reach the place of forgiveness, you have to acknowledge that your dark side would much rather slit her throat! Embracing that desire doesn't mean you'll act on it. All it does is open the space for you to move past your jealousy, forgive her, and if you're lucky maybe even get to see that jealousy is based in the fear that love is scarce.

All of us have a Shadow aspect and if we want to be free to experience our selves to the fullest we have to be willing to look it straight in the eye and say, "What's going on?" If you don't, life will leave a bad taste in your mouth. When we're young, we're heavily programmed to believe that being up and happy all the time is the only socially acceptable way to be. We go on for years suppressing all of our darker emotions, thinking we're doing everyone a favor. When we hit menopause, much of what we never wanted to look at rises to the surface whether we want it to or not. People call it bitchiness or hormonal insanity, but it only remains so if we allow it to lie unexamined. The truth about our dark side, or our Shadow Self, is that 50 percent of our creativity and capacity for fulfillment is stored there. To deny or suppress it is to shut ourselves off to the vast reserves of wisdom and emotional strength that are held in that part of our psyche. When we overcome the fear that attends the idea of examining our darker feelings, we open up to the possibility of bringing them out into the light and *loving* them. Once we *see* and *know* what's there, it no longer has any power over us.

Reclaiming and owning the Shadow aspect of our nature allows us to consciously integrate it into the totality of who we are. Through it we become *whole*. Being whole and complete within yourself is what the wisdom of the Crone is all about. If we choose *not* to do this, all that darkness stays locked within. The problem is, it doesn't go away. Oh no! All that messed-up energy runs our lives like an invisible iron fist, and it keeps us bitchy, bitter, and unfulfilled. I don't know about you, but I would certainly rather come to terms with my s___ than allow it to ruin what's left of my life. And once you get the hang of what it really means to go into those dark spaces in your heart, you see how empowering it is to reconnect with yourself in that way. A fully balanced, well-integrated, older female is a dynamo. And what we're here for, girls, whether you know it or not, is to transmit all our power out into the world so that the males and everyone else on the planet can figure out how to function the way the Great Spirit and the Great Mother intended them to. If all of us "Old Girls" really knew how incredible we were and acted accordingly, the whole world would light up.

This "introduction" is a little longer than I intended it to be, and what I want to say next is kind of off the subject but not really. It's well known in spiritual circles that the power on the planet got handed over to the female back in 1987–1988. I don't know if you remember the Harmonic Convergence, but during that time, in a sacred ceremony at Lake Titicaca, the male forces that had held control over the Earth for close to 13,000 years passed the torch on to the feminine principle. Events like this never make it into the papers, but there are archetypal energies greater than our own that take care of things behind the scenes in regular cycles. Thank God they're on the ball!

Sixteen years later, here we are. Those of us who got popped out onto the planet during the baby boom are spiritual forerunners. We're here to set an example for every woman-child who comes after us. Ours is the first generation of women who didn't buy into what the patriarchal forces were trying to sell us. It's up to us to restore the role of the Elder Female to a state of grace and respect. Now that we're old enough to know who we are, we need to go deeper, we need to go beyond the veil and see what lies there. Unwinding the tangled cords that hold the Shadow Self in bondage will reveal what a few of us have already begun to get a grip on: Life is incredible. And it gets better as you get older. Being a Grandmother is awesome, just like the word implies–richer and more powerful than being a Mom. If we do our homework, it'll make life a hell of a lot easier for our daughters, and their daughters, and for all the males on the planet too.

When my publisher and I first started talking about what we were going to do for my second book, we were going call it *The Old Girls' Book of Shadows*. It was my brainchild, and both of us saw it as a sequel to my first book, *The Old Girls' Book of Spells*. I liked the idea of doing a Book of Shadows because I am a witch, and any witch worth her salt has a Book of Shadows. A Book of Shadows is a place to record your spell work. Every time you do magic you bring all kinds of elements together: planetary and lunar rhythms, different herbs, oils, and measurements. Some of these will work like a charm and some of them won't yield much result. Results are what count when you're a serious witch, so it's good to keep a record of what works and what doesn't. A Book of Shadows is a lot like a bunch of recipes that you've tested. Over time you build an arsenal of knowledge that you can refer to and modify over and over again.

But I didn't want the title of this book to make it seem as if *only* women who are into Wicca would benefit from reading it. That's why we settled instead on *The Old Girls' Book of Dreams*. After all, dreams and shadows are sort of the same. The Shadow Self is at the wheel when we're in the dreamtime. And in real time, if you don't reckon with your Shadow Self it makes it nearly impossible to manifest *any* of your dreams.

Those of you who are into the Craft may already have a Book of Shadows. If you don't, let this be it. I have every spell I've ever done tucked safely away in a leatherbound book that a good friend of mine made for me a long time ago. This book is like a magical Bible that I've used over the years. The knowledge in it is priceless because it comes from my own experience, and there is nothing like it in the world. Whether you're a veteran witch or just getting started with Wicca, what you write in this Book of Dreams will become as precious to you as my Book of Shadows is to me.

Even if you're not into Wicca, life is magical, and all of us are witches. You may not be hot on the idea of doing spells, but if you're reading this book chances are you've got more on your mind than what to add to the meat loaf tonight to make it taste better! I think most of us got meat loaf down ages ago and have graduated to life's deeper mysteries. *All* of us have stuff going on in our hearts and our minds. What we do to handle it varies from person to person. So use this Book of Dreams to record what happens in your attempts to create what you want and wish for. As you get more comfortable with what it means to make your dreams real, the pages of this book will offer you a place to look back on what happens as they come true. If life is driving you crazy and you just need a place to vent, use it for that. This may be the only place where your Shadow Self gets any airtime. Use the time you spend writing on these pages to seed your dreams and connect with whatever is going on with you.

I've chosen to arrange this book of dreams according to the Zodiac cycle because I'm an astrologer and a witch and it's how I relate to time. The Gregorian Calendar introduced by Pope Gregory in 1582 was a patriarchal "invention." It is totally out of synch with the natural flow of the earth's movement through space relative to the Sun and the path it traces through the greater universe. I have spent years watching the earth move in relation to the Sun and the Moon and the stars. The rhythm of the cosmos is impossible to miss if you're paying attention. It's that rhythm that I choose to honor because I not only know, I feel that I am a part of it and I have not forgotten that I am connected to it. The whole purpose of this book is to help everyone who reads it understand how to make their dreams come alive. You can't tune in to that process if you're using a system of time division that doesn't even recognize what's taking place in the natural world! And because we're living in a time when our memory of who we really are is finally being restored, using the Zodiac cycle to mark time in this book makes more sense to me.

The book begins with Capricorn, but that doesn't mean that you have to start using it in January! Start anywhere in the year—the month you begin reading it; at your own Sun sign; anywhere you feel inspired. Pick it up and put it down again, or work your way through it. Take years if you need to.

I've included reflections at the top of each page, and they are there to take in and respond to if you wish. It's fine by me if you totally disregard them, but they may provide you with a jumping-off point if you're at a loss for words or have no spells to cast. Life is serendipitous and everything is in divine order, so whatever the reflection is, chances are it will apply to what's happening with you from day to day. Even if it doesn't, it'll give you something to laugh or cry or think about. Some of these little words of wisdom have been culled from the writings and spoken words of well-known and anonymous wise women. Most of them have been spun out of my own experiences; many have come out of conversations I've had with people who mean a lot to me. My friends are my teachers, and whenever we talk we go to the heart of things. All kinds of enlightening revelations rise to the surface whenever two or more gather and go to the heart space.

At the beginning of this introduction, I promised that I'd tell you how you could get into your "heart space." This technique was taught to me by Drunvalo Melchizedek who is an amazing being and a wonderful teacher deeply committed to raising the consciousness of humanity and to healing the problems that Mother Earth is facing at this time. He travels all over the world disseminating the Flower of Life teachings and training people in MerKaBa Meditation. I have been using his "heart space" technique for more than two years, and it has changed my life completely.

First you need to find enough peace and quiet to sit down and close your eyes for at least half an hour. Slow your breathing down, and with your mind visualize your head separate from your body. Mentally set it up above your body as if it's temporarily sitting on a shelf. It's important to do this so that your mind can't interfere with what you're about to do. (Don't worry, when you're finished you will reattach your head.)

Now bring your consciousness to the opening at the top of your neck, and when you feel ready, slowly move your consciousness and your awareness down into your throat. Feel and sense yourself inside your throat, and keep moving down into your sternum and chest area until you get to where your heart is. See yourself standing in front of your heart and get a feel for it as a physical organ. This will be different for each of you, and it doesn't matter what you see in your inner vision. There is no wrong way to do this.

When you know it's time to enter your heart you can do one of two things: You can enter directly by slipping through the outer wall of the heart, or you can go in through the top. There is a doughnut-shaped energy field around the heart that circulates in and out through the top and the bottom. If you choose this route, all you have to do is pour your consciousness in through the vortex at the top and it will spiral down inside the heart. Whichever route you take, when you get into the heart it will probably be very dark. If it is, ask for the light to come. When the light comes you will find yourself in the heart chamber. This chamber will appear different to each of you. It's a space that your soul is well familiar with. It's where you go between each and every one of your lifetimes. Inside this chamber you can do anything. You can ask any question and receive the answer. You can invite anyone you wish to communicate with into the heart space and talk to them in any way you want. If you listen they will answer you. If you have a desire and wish to create something you can do it from this place. It doesn't matter whether it's something personal or if it's something that you would like to see happen at a planetary level. You can do anything you want when you're in the heart chamber.

For those of you who are saying to yourselves, "This is crazy, give me a break!" I have something to tell you: The heart has its own consciousness. Keep in mind that when a fetus develops, the heart starts beating before the brain is even formed. This implies that some force exists inside the heart that causes it to begin pulsing. That force is pure consciousness, and it is unaffected by the polarity that is intrinsic to the mind. When you create from inside the heart, your dreams will manifest exactly the way you intend them to with no negative result. And don't worry about whether these instructions will be used destructively by people who wish for power and control. The heart is a soft, female place. You'll feel this when you go there. *Only* what is of the light can exist in that place. When you're creating your dreams you can stay in your heart chamber for as long as you want. Incredible things happen, and you won't want to leave!

If you have trouble doing this process it's because you've experienced so much emotional trauma that all those memories are in the way. If that is the case, keep trying! Whatever's in the way will eventually yield to your efforts. To support these efforts, find a good energy healer and allow her to help you release those memories.

When you feel like you're ready to return to the world, leave your heart the way you entered it and slowly move up through your chest area to your throat again. Feel yourself inside your throat for a few moments. Then, in your inner vision, bring your head back to your neck and reattach it. It is very important to follow this step to the letter. After all you need your mind to function in 3D and you can't leave it hanging around on the etheric plane! Whenever you have anything you wish to create, heal, or dream into being, you can enter the heart chamber via either of the routes I've described and use this technique. Amazing things will take place every time you do this.

I hope you will use this book to weave your dreams and let them take you closer to wherever your path is leading you. Use it for magic or whatever your heart desires. But when you die, make sure you pass your book on to your girls. Maybe it will help them see that what a woman gets out of life is in direct proportion to her ability to dream.

CAPRICORN
December 21–January 20

A dvent and the joyful expectancy that fills it lead us up to the Winter Solstice. The first day of winter is magical because it marks the return of the Sun. It's also the start of the coldest, hardest part of the year. And while the light is definitely increasing, the fact that we're freezing our asses off is much more obvious. The shift into Capricorn is a heavy-duty reality check, and even though the holidays distract us momentarily, the truth is that at this point in the cycle we get back to square one. Saturn is the archetypal ruler of Capricorn. All the old etchings of Saturn depict him as "The Grim Reaper"—the guy who shows up when death is at the door and reminds us that we're mortal. The bottom line is that we're all going to die someday. Dying may be the harshest reality we face, but life and death go hand in hand, and every ending is a doorway to a new beginning. If you have doubts about this, keep your eye on the Sun. Through some sort of miracle it comes back to life on the longest, darkest night of the year.

Back when the Christians took over they had to wean the Pagans off their habit of celebrating the Winter Solstice, so to ease the transition they told everyone Christ was born on December 25. The Christians knew that the Pagans celebrated the return of the Oak King on December 21, and they figured that whoever they converted would be happier about it if they had a suitable replacement for their King. So the conquerors hoodwinked all the locals into thinking that the star of this new show was distantly related to the Oak King by starting the rumor that Jesus was born right near the Solstice. Jesus was actually a Pisces. But the former Pagans went along with the program because they were naïve and because they would have been slaughtered if they didn't.

All that aside, the real cause for rejoicing in mid-December is the fact that the solar light is returning. Between now and the Vernal Equinox every day will contain *one more minute* of sunlight.

I am pretty sure that when they repackaged the Winter Solstice rituals, they invented New Year's too. And poor us! Since then we've had to live with the insanity created by this ruse. Before our hangovers are even gone we have to get happy about turning over a new leaf! Though it may be appropriate to begin thinking about what's next, at the coldest, darkest point in the year, someone please tell me, who's got the energy for it? With the IRS breathing down our necks, ten extra pounds on our hips, and three feet of snow on the ground, crawling back under the covers with what's left of the holiday chocolates sounds more attractive to me.

You'll be happy to know that I'm not here to crack the whip or tell you to get on the ball. Pep talks aren't my thing. And I've learned over time that the more you try to control things the less control you have. Any effort to whip yourself into shape only feeds the idea that you're out of control. And if there's a thought form that says you're out of control, guess what? You will be. Life at this point in the year is more about hibernating, and if you make any attempt to resist what Nature is obviously calling you to do you'll flunk out this semester.

When I think about Capricorn I picture an uptight business-man in a three-piece suit. And on the surface Capricorn *is* all business. It's a very male frequency, totally in charge and in control. If this is so then why the hell is Mother Earth in a coma right now? Why is she sleeping under a blanket of snow when the archetypal influences that currently rule her are into taking care of business? In 3D, everything exists in relation to its opposite. Capricorn's polar opposite is the sign Cancer, the Woman-Mother who nurtures and protects. She doesn't force her will on *anything* and is more concerned with giving birth and making love than with squeezing into her pantyhose and running off to work. The reason Mother Earth sleeps through the winter is because she needs the rest. *Duh!* She has no strength for outer things, and she's in tune enough with who she is to just say, "F____ it!" when she wants to.

We're no different than the Great Mother and could learn a lot by following her rhythms. Whatever we need to be doing outwardly isn't going to fly if we don't have a really healthy inner connection. So, I highly recommend curling up somewhere with a good book and a cup of tea whenever you feel like it. Don't worry too much about your ability to manage external pressures this month. Even the animals know enough to hibernate when it's cold out. Crawl back under the covers. Sleep as much as you can. Feed yourself when you need to and nurture the little baby girl inside you. The reward you gain from slowing everything down will yield incredible results. And whatever you birth inside yourself will be the foundation for all the wonderful things that come to life because you took the time to do it.

What did you think was supposed to happen?
Where did that idea come from?

....

....

....

....

....

....

....

....

....

....

....

....

....

....

....

....

....

I hate, loathe, and despise Christmas. It's a time when single people have to take cover or get out of town.

–KRISTIN HUNTER, *The Landlord* (1966)

Don't get too hung up trying to control things. It takes all the fun out of life.

You may not like what's happening but it won't change
until you do.

In a way winter is the real spring, the time when the inner thing happens, the resurge of nature.

—EDNA O'BRIEN, *Mrs. Reinhardt* (1978)

Sometimes a nap puts everything in perspective.

Listen to the voice that speaks to you from the inside.
It knows exactly what you need to do.

If I had the strength I would just do nothing.
–KATHARINA SPURLING

Perhaps I am a bear, or some hibernating animal, underneath, for the instinct to be half asleep all winter is so strong in me.

—ANNE MORROW LINDBERGH, *Bring Me a Unicorn* (1971)

You are not your body, your baggage, or your stuff.

Just turn your light on. Let it shine, and never doubt whether it will remove the darkness.

The etiquette question that troubles so many fastidious people New Year's Day is: How am I ever going to face those people again?

–JUDITH MARTIN, *Miss Manners' Guide to Excruciatingly Correct Behavior* (1982)

AQUARIUS
January 21–February 20

When I was younger this time of year used to depress me. I pushed myself through it by fueling up with tons of calories and reminding myself that it was only going to last a few weeks. Taking off for the tropics wasn't in the budget. Having money in the winter meant getting Fuel Assistance at Cal's house! My daughter Eliza was born on Valentine's Day, so halfway through at least there was *that* to get happy about. Too bad I'm not one of those women who ever wanted to know what Victoria's Secret was. The Hearts and Flowers that are supposed to light your fire on Valentine's Day never got me going. It's just as well. The men in my life have either been cheap and practical or cross-addicted, macho cavemen, and if we celebrated on the 14th of February it was by turning up the heat, one way or another.

Maybe it's a godsend that my personal life has been such a disaster. Instead of whining about it I got into my studies and my spiritual work. Astrology and the Wiccan ways have turned Aquarius into my favorite month. I see it in a completely different light now that I'm a Crone. Nature teaches me everything I need to know, and I've spent many winters watching Mother Earth and Father Sky do their winter dance. Look around. The world is covered with ice, the air is filled with crystals, and everything is locked in a state of suspended animation. The life force in the frozen ground is hibernating, and there's not a trace of evidence that it will revive. The stark background that we conduct our lives against provides us with plenty of opportunity to see only what is essential. With nothing to distract us, we have plenty of time to ponder. What are we here for? What do we really want? What are our ideals and are they working for us? Do they need to change? The dead of winter is the perfect time to reevaluate everything that we're doing so that we can be reborn with a new vision in the spring.

The sign Aquarius is the embodiment of the Visionary arche-type. The frequency that vibrates through the Unified Field when the Sun is in this sign endows everything in it with the capacity to dream. Everyone knows that when we dream we wish for or envision possibilities that don't exist. What we know less about is the fact that if you hold your dreams in your heart for any length of time they become real. The importance of the dream and the strength of the wish bring it to life. It doesn't matter what the dream is. You can wish for a Mercedes-Benz or you can hold a vision that all the people of the world will remember what it means to live in peace and harmony. Dreams are the matrix that reality is woven upon. If we're too fearful to strike out and carve new para-digms or don't understand the importance of weaving new and better visions, the structures we create become static and wind up choking us to death.

In the Wiccan traditions February 2 is an important cross-quarter. The four major cross-quarters are the two Solstice points and the Vernal and Autumnal Equinox points. The midpoints between those dates mark the four "lesser" cross-quarters and February 2 is one of them. These eight days mark points in time when the "veil" that separates the world of spirit from the world of men is so thin that a cosmic portal opens up. What comes through each portal is pure cosmic energy and that energy is there to be tapped. If you know how to plug in to it you can use it to super charge whatever you desire at the moment. February 2 is known as Imbolc, Saint Brigid's Day, or Candlemas, depending on where you're from. God knows what they were thinking, but when the patriarchal forces extinguished the Old Ways they renamed this holy day Groundhog Day! Why they stuck such a stupid label on one of the most magical points in the year is beyond me.

People's lives were much more intimately twined with Nature in the old days, and mid-winter must have been the pits. Supplies were low, food was scarce, and no one knew how harsh the remainder of the season would be. But every year on February 2 the ewes started lactating. They still do, by the way, and have every year since the dawn of time. This was the sign that something was "quickening" inside Mother Earth and that her womb was preparing to bring forth new life. *Imbolc* means "in the belly." Saint Brigid is an ancient fertility goddess. She was brought up by a wizard and became quite a magician herself. Her specialty was the ability to multiply food and drink. Candlemas is about light, and all the rituals performed on February 2 involve lighting candles to pierce the winter darkness.

The various traditions associated with this cross-quarter could fill a book. *All* of them are incredibly beautiful and real. Behind every one of them the intention is the same: to seed the dreams for whatever we want to come to life in the spring. On the eve of February 2 I sit with a white candle and a pitcher of fresh milk and think about what I really want. When the vision is clear I walk outside and pour the milk into the snow and watch it flow down into the frozen ground. As this happens I see all of my wishes coming true. And by the Spring Equinox these visions begin to manifest, showing me that there's more to the Old Ways than meets the eye.

Use this month to dream new dreams. Watch and see what happens to them, and keep in mind, you *can* have *anything* you want.

....

....

....

....

....

....

....

....

....

....

....

....

....

....

....

....

....

....

....

....

 What would you do right now if you could do anything you want?

Our beliefs shape us. We are what we believe.

Like all people who have nothing, I lived on dreams.

—ANZIA YEZIERSKA, *Hungry Hearts* (1920)

If wishes were horses, then beggars would ride.
Well, saddle up, honey.

–ANONYMOUS

What is up with men? No matter how long I live I will never understand them.

The worst times eventually turn out to be the best times.

This earth is my sister. . . .

—SUSAN GRIFFIN, *Woman and Nature* (1978)

The only reason you're here is to be who you are.

Do you know what you want?

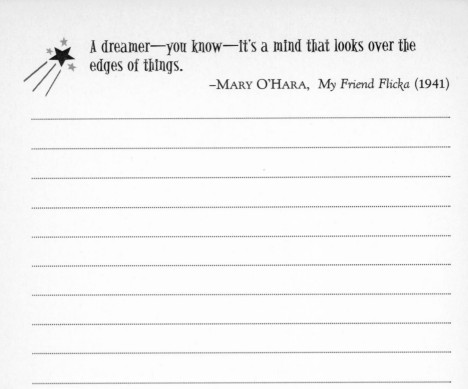

A dreamer—you know—it's a mind that looks over the edges of things.

–MARY O'HARA, *My Friend Flicka* (1941)

I dream, therefore I become.

         –CHERYL GROSSMAN, *button* (1989)

I used to meditate to make it easier to cope. Now I meditate because it opens up a pathway to the part of myself that knows my true purpose here. Regardless of how my personality is coping, all that I really want is to serve that purpose.

PISCES
February 21–March 20

U p where I live in southern Vermont, it's cabin fever time. Being cooped up all winter definitely makes you feel like you're in the Twilight Zone, and every year I think, "What if Rod Serling is behind all of this? What would life be like if winter never came to an end?" Cabin fever may be about the huge cosmic transition that's taking place at this time during the year; like any transition, it's a death of sorts. The Sun is in Pisces till the 20th of March. Pisces is at the tail end of the Zodiac, so everything that was initiated in the previous cycle has run its course. Any death is also a new begin-ning, but before we can be reborn we have to release what's unfolded over the last 365 days. It's appropriate that the symbol for Pisces is the image of two fish swimming in opposite directions. And we get that squirrelly feeling at this time of year because, like the two fish, we don't know if we're coming or going. Why would we? We're smack in the middle of this huge void, floating in some sort of purgatory, running totally on faith that the light will return one more time and melt the winter darkness.

Cabin fever doesn't get to me anymore. I love Vermont when the Sun's in Pisces because the sap starts running and all the Woodchucks are out tapping the trees. For those of you that don't know what a "Woodchuck" is, it's a term we use up here to label a guy who works physically hard, wears buffalo-checked wool shirts, doesn't shave, isn't into gun control, and didn't go to Harvard. These men are a hell of a lot smarter than they look but you'd never know it because they don't talk a lot and their wisdom isn't intellectual. I have a terminal weakness for Woodchucks. It's been the bane of my existence that I am *only* attracted to this type of guy. My poor mother still can't figure it out. Neither can I. And it doesn't matter, because I didn't bring them up to talk about my taste in men.

These guys work like dogs to begin with, but the moment the Sun moves into Pisces they spend every spare minute hauling sap out of the woods. What quickens inside Mother Earth's belly in February triggers off something mysterious that causes her juices to flow. By the time March hits she's out of control. There's no way to stop this liquid, and these men make countless trips in and out of the forest at all hours of the day and night just to retrieve it and transform it into syrup. The sexual metaphor is so obvious here I don't need to point it out but I can't leave it alone. Herds of males running in and out of the bushes to service this gigantic female who's totally aroused and ready to go. It's so sexy. And once they've collected all this juice they heat it up over huge fires and stand around watching as it turns into something sweet and heavenly. Maybe I'm losing it, but I wonder how good the syrup would be if the male frequency wasn't there to stir it? If the Woodchucks had any clue that what they were engaged in had sexual overtones they'd probably do it naked. I have a feeling they don't see it quite the way I do. For them the sap run is more like having a big slot machine in the woods that keeps hitting the jack-pot. As far as they're concerned, what they make off their syrup keeps the wolf from the door.

The fact that Mother Nature turns herself on year after year blows me away. I am totally in awe that she knows what to do, and I worship her ability to do it. I drive the roads in February and March, and as soon as I see the boys out and the smoke curling up out of the sap houses I get psyched. If you live in the city you don't notice this stuff, but around here you can't help it. And I get excited because these signs tell me that all the dreams I seeded back in February are coming alive. They remind me that the Twilight Zone is just a temporary stop, not a permanent destination, and that winter *will* end one more time, just like it always has. If you feel like you're in limbo right now, consider it normal and keep the faith. The flow of energy that will carry your dreams up to the surface of your life is on its way. This force will rise the same way the sap rises and the same way the waters of the womb have to break before anything new can be born.

Men are all wonderful; they just don't know it.

The mind has only questions. The heart has only answers.

Each of us has a purpose. Finding out what yours is is what you're here for.

You can continue to be right about the way things are or you can do what it takes to get the results you want in your life.

The reward of patience is patience.

When I dream
I am always ageless.

–ELIZABETH COATSWORTH, *Personal Geography* (1976)

I wouldn't want to be young again. I love being old.

The Earth is your Mother. Love her. She's the source of everything.

I used to be furious with Mummy, and still am sometimes. It's true that she doesn't understand me, but I don't understand her either.

—ANNE FRANK, *The Diary of a Young Girl* (1952)

41

The footsteps your kids follow in are the ones you thought you covered up.

—ANONYMOUS

....

....

....

....

....

....

....

....

....

....

....

....

....

....

....

....

....

....

....

It's unbelievable the primitive feelings that are aroused by rapid change.

–SHEILA BALLANTYNE, *Norma Jean the Termite Queen* (1975)

A powerful woman isn't a female trying to act like a guy. Feminine strength is a whole different thing. It comes from inside.

ARIES
March 21–April 20

I look forward to the Spring Equinox more than I do my birthday. The anticipation comes from I don't know what. Maybe it's because the male vibration is all over the place. And I literally feel like I'm sixteen years old, sitting on the front porch, waiting for this gorgeous guy to show up and remind me what being a woman is all about. Spring fever hits *everyone* like a ton of bricks. And it's because the internal stuff that goes on all winter ripens on the first day of spring. It's so interesting to me that schoolkids and those of us who still like to play take an egg out of the fridge at the Equinox just to see if it really *will* stand up by itself on the kitchen counter. This experiment is so symbolic: this Ovum is the end result of all the inner, female work it took a winter to process. And on the 21st of March whatever we've done inside has reached a point where it *has* to be balanced by a force equal but opposite to its own or it will not develop any further. Female energy alone is not enough, even though many of us would like to think it is. The creation process has a male aspect, too, and that male aspect shows up in all his glory the *moment* the Sun moves into Aries. So after four months of being whole and complete within ourselves all of a sudden there's this "guy" energy permeating the universal matrix. And the *only* thing this archetypal guy is interested in is getting laid! He's not being crude and boorish; he's doing what comes naturally to him because that's his function. We may fool ourselves into thinking that we need to fend him off and be ladylike but deep inside we know better. The truth is we don't want to. If this "egg" we've created isn't impregnated soon, the dreams we've been nurturing ain't gonna go nowhere. That's all there is to it.

It must be time to talk about sex. I have been working on my Ph.D. in this area since I was fifteen and I still know practically nothing about it. There's a lot of conversation that sex goes down the tubes after the change. This is a lie that's very easy to buy into. Our mothers may have said things, and if you've been with the same guy for eons, having sex with him may be as enticing to you as going to the dentist. If you've had a lot of men there's been more variety, but mass quantities of phallic energy don't necessarily add up to much. (If you're gay, please forgive me for not including you in this discussion. I have no clue what the sexual dynamics are for gay women, but I have a feeling we could learn a lot from you.) At this point in my "research" my understanding of sex is that the male gets his power not by getting off but by being in the presence of the force that awakens in the female when she is in a state of ecstasy. And it serves him to keep her in this state as often and as much as possible because it's his power source; the more he's around it the more empowering it is for him on every level of his Being. The reason most middle-aged males are bored stiff sexually or strung out on Viagra is that they're oblivious to this secret. Imagine what life would be like in the bedroom if they knew about it. Us girls would be in heaven and probably on our knees willing to do *anything* for the man in bed or out! And the man would be so invigorated by the end-less waves of energy coming out from inside the female he'd want sex all the time. Talk about a win-win situation!

If you're one of those women who's never had an orgasm, what are you waiting for? Stop whatever you're doing and figure it out. Practice makes perfect! Every body has the same equipment. If it's your mental stuff that keeps you from surrendering, look at what it's costing you and give it up! Sex is important and it's not separate from the rest of your life. Any imbalance there throws everything else off-kilter. Every time you have an orgasm every cell in your body gets rejuvenated. We tell ourselves, "We're getting old, we're wrinkled and fat, it's all over for us in the sex department." Bullshit! We get old, wrinkled, and fat as soon as we start to believe this. I'd love to get my hands on whoever sold us the myth that women don't need or want sex after menopause. If anything we need to have more of it.

It's spring fever time. Do something sexy. Bring that male energy in. And when you come up for air, remember, the dreams you've been stirring for the last four months won't go anywhere if you don't surrender them to the universe. Something needs to spark those visions up, and the male force that takes over the Unified Field when the Sun moves into Aries is there to fertilize them. There are countless ways to be orgasmic—in all parts of your life. Whatever you conjured up back in February will begin to take form if you allow it to come out. So go sit on the porch (sit any-where you like!), and let Nature take its course.

Every day when you wake up say, "God, I love my life!"

....

....

....

....

....

....

....

....

....

....

....

....

....

....

....

It's not the men in my life that counts, it's the life in my men.

—MAE WEST, in *I'm No Angel* (1933)

Being in love is a state of mind that makes it impossible to think about anything else.

_____

_____

_____

_____

_____

_____

_____

_____

_____

_____

_____

_____

_____

_____

_____

_____

_____

_____

 If you're feeling a little too ordinary don't let it get you down. Think of it this way; you're so ordinary, you're **extra** ordinary.

Sexuality is a sacrament.
—STARHAWK, *The Spiral Dance* (1979)

Everyone should have at least one affair before they die.

Be smart enough to know what isn't your business.

When I was young I didn't know I was beautiful.
Now that I'm old I'm totally clear about it, but nobody
notices anymore.

At the Turning of the Ages women are the ones who hold the power. It's up to us to lead the way. Men are so heavily programmed to believe that they're in charge they don't listen. Have the courage to speak your truth and in time they will have the courage to follow you.

Don't be embarrassed or self-conscious.
There's no wrong way to do anything.

From God's perspective nothing is intrinsically wrong. What's wrong for anyone is that which causes feelings of remorse.

Our visions begin with our desires.

–Audre Lord

TAURUS
April 21–May 20

Y ou don't need a calendar to tell you when the Sun moves into
Taurus. It's the day the grass turns green. I have been keeping
track of this phenomenon for years, and I've seen it happen over
and over again. The fiery, masculine force that permeated the
ethers while the Sun was in Aries has done its work. Now, whatever we want to bring to fruition has to be grounded and stabilized
in things that are real. After all, this is a sensate universe. If we
can't perceive the reality of our dreams with our senses, we have
no proof that they exist. The greening of the grass is the first sign
that Mother Earth is totally OK with holding and growing whatever the male wishes to fill her with. As the next few weeks
unfold, her response to this will become more and more apparent.
Spring fever may have begun at the Equinox but it's running full
tilt when the Sun's in Taurus. And the sixteen-year-old girl who
was sitting on the front porch has by now been courted enough by
the male to *know* that her beauty is without question. She no longer
wonders if she is beautiful and is out to strut her stuff. Look
around. You can see it everywhere. By April 30 or the 1st of May
there will be a green fire of leaves budding on the trees bursting on
every hillside. The rivers will be full, with cool, clear water cours-
ing down from the mountains of melting snow. Tulips and crocuses
will push their way up through the soft, brown earth. All this

incredible beauty will be proof that what we have been wanting is here at last, showing itself to our senses for the first time.

One of the most important Pagan cross-quarters happens this month. The forty-eight hours between April 30 and May 1 is known as Beltane. Beltane is an old fertility and fire ritual. Huge bonfires used to light up the hillsides on the eve of May 1, and people would take turns jumping over them to insure fecundity, longevity, lasting love, or whatever. They'd drive their herds through the ashes of these fires to make sure milk, meat, and wool would be plentiful. The Pagan people knew that the veil that separates the world of Spirit from the world of Nature is very thin on Beltane Eve. And they used this time to literally "ground" everything they wanted and wished for into the earth. Everyone would go out into the woods and mate with whoever they wanted to. Wanton lust may have been the motivating factor, but they believed, too, that free love would bring life to whatever they did between May and the end of October. The Old Ways and all forms of nature worship were 86'd when the Christians took over. Saint Patrick made it clear that Christianity was boss in the year 433. Everyone knew what it meant when he usurped the power of the High King by lighting the first Beltane Fire. If what the Pagan people did seems barbaric to us, it's only because we've been entrained by generations of puritanical programming to see it that way. We may be more civilized than they were, but I have a feeling they were better off. It seems more joyful and honest to take pleasure in the fact that we're human than it does to suppress the idea and have to live with what happens when the sexual instincts get twisted. In my mind, pornography, perversion, and pedophilia are a hell of a lot more barbaric than outdoor sex on a spring night.

This coming month is extremely powerful. All of us would be wise to take our cue from Mother Nature. Get in touch with your own beauty and recognize your femaleness enough to let it show. Bring everything you have within you out into the open, and allow it to form a direct connection with something positive. We have to root our dreams firmly in the soil of our lives so they will find a way to grow. Be more sexual if you want to. The male and female polarities *need* to be balanced for anything to happen. It may help you to understand what it is you are wanting if you let those waves of energy come out from inside you and enter the Unified Field. Female energy is magnetic. If you let that force vibrate, it will attract something electric. Even if all you do is connect with your own Animus, you will become actively engaged in making things happen.

Pull yourself together and get as real as you can about what's important in your life. What do you want to manifest between now and the end of October? Use Beltane to bring it into focus. Go out and get your garden planted. And with every seed you sow, keep in mind that it holds much more than whatever's in its DNA. Your dreams are there too. And I guarantee that when you look back at what you do this month, every single one of those dreams will have come true.

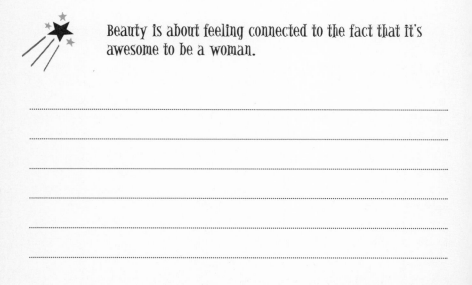

Beauty is about feeling connected to the fact that it's awesome to be a woman.

A little Madness in the Spring
Is wholesome even for the King.

—Emily Dickinson,
in Martha Dickinson Bianchi, ed., *The Single Hound* (1914)

When was the last time you got laid?

Sex is an emotion in motion.

–Mae West (1965)

Every time you have an orgasm every cell in your body lights up.

Saddle your dreams afore you ride 'em.

         –MARY WEBB, *Precious Bane* (1924)

Love your body.

You cannot escape sex. It will track you to
the ends of the earth.

—JAN CLAUSEN, *Mother, Sister, Daughter, Lover* (1980)

Don't complicate sex by trying too hard to be sexy.

The problem is the seed for the answer to it.

People need dreams, there's as much nourishment in 'em as food.

–DOROTHY GILMAN, *Caravan* (1992)

....

....

....

....

....

....

....

....

....

....

....

....

....

....

....

....

....

 Being in touch with your feminine side requires you to be playful, joyful, and receptive. Sounds like fun to me!

GEMINI
May 21–June 20

Everything starts moving very quickly at this time in the yearly cycle. All the kids get out of school, people take off on vacation, there's more freedom to move around, and a restless vibration causes us to want to get out of wherever we are and go all over the place. The dreams that we grounded at Beltane are secure by now and strong enough to stand on their own. Staying rooted to one spot serves a purpose, but it's counterproductive from an evolutionary perspective because anything can come along and break your stem or knock you down. And if we don't find a way to integrate our visions into the larger universe, what's the point of having them? The commencement exercises and graduation ceremonies that take place throughout the next month are a sign that *all* of us have to graduate to the next level. So it's time to take your show on the road, girls. These dreams need to find their niche.

Late May and early June are as filled with promise as a senior at graduation. All options are open. It's like having diplomatic license plates, because "we're out of school" and the only rules we're subject to are the ones we make for ourselves. Knowing that you have cosmic permission to do whatever you want is so awesome. You can keep moving along in the direction you've chosen if that makes you happy. You can change directions too. Anything goes. I find it interesting that we live in a culture where focus and persistence get such high ratings. The ability to be free and flexible is just as valuable, and right now in the creation process it's mandatory. Whatever we were aiming for could easily be missed if we're too rigid about where the arrow goes. And the possibilities may include things that we never even considered. If we want to access all possibilities, we have to lighten up.

The sign Gemini rules this month. I hate to say it, but I'm kind of an intellectual elitist, and I have always been a real snob about Gemini energy. It's way too light for me. I read *The Secret Doctrine*, I'm into the occult, and I never watch TV or go to parties. Parties bore me. Geminis aren't like this. They want to do everything, and it's all the same to them. They're extremely clever, curious people, and they know a little about a lot of things. If you try to get too into their stuff or want the conversation to get deep and meaningful, forget about it; they turn the channel. I have never been able to figure out whether they're holding back or if the sacred mysteries and the ultimate answers just don't matter to them. But as I have gotten older, I've learned that keeping things light has its place. Though Geminis may need to go deeper, I definitely need to stop being so serious. When you're too serious it's impossible to have fun. And if you don't know how to have fun you can't be joyful. "Play mode" is where it's at this month. The ability to take delight in everything makes it possible to taste it all and discover what gives us joy.

When I was a kid, this month was vacation time. We'd pack up the station wagon and head for Maine. My sisters and I used to walk up and down the beach all day long collecting seashells. And if we got tired of that we'd fill buckets with periwinkles and hermit crabs and move on to making drip castles in the sand. In between we'd play in the waves and make pit stops at Mum's blanket for peanut butter and jelly sandwiches. We spent weeks at a time with no sense of purpose, doing nothing in particular, and never got tired of it. Looking back on this, it's clear to me that we were all in an altered state. I see now that I was nothing more than a little atomic particle spinning and vibrating within a larger matrix of other particles that were joyfully doing the same thing. And nothing we did was important, but somehow or other all of it was important because we were there contributing to it and connected to it.

I have been looking for God all of my life. I have searched for him everywhere. And I laugh now as I realize that I was probably closer to him as a small child on the beach than I have ever been since. Miraculous things happen when you shift out of the gears that supposedly pull you forward. When you're in play mode your entire C is in a state of praise. Just the fact that you exist and are free to let your consciousness merge with whatever is out there makes everything fascinating and all things possible. It's time for your dreams to fly wherever they need to go to fulfill themselves. So put on your diplomatic license plates. Gently tell your ego, your agendas, and the illusion that anything matters to vacate the premises. For God to come through and guide you to the place where your visions will light up, all you really need to do is be a child.

Be like a child and look at everything with wonder.

You can't evolve spiritually if you still think that some people are better than others.

What one loves in childhood lives in the heart forever.

—MARY JO PUTNEY, *Silk and Secrets* (1992)

All happiness is a form of innocence.
—MARGUERITE YOURCENAR, Alexis (1929)

People are all crazy no matter how they look.

Stop being bummed out about your age.

Don't be in such a hurry. Time is an illusion like everything else.

Try not to judge people, or anything for that matter.

A daydreamer is prepared for most things.
—JOYCE CAROL OATES, *The Wheel of Love (1969)*

_____

_____

_____

_____

_____

_____

_____

_____

_____

_____

_____

_____

_____

_____

_____

_____

_____

 Life is fluid. If you want to stay on top of things you need to learn how to walk on water.

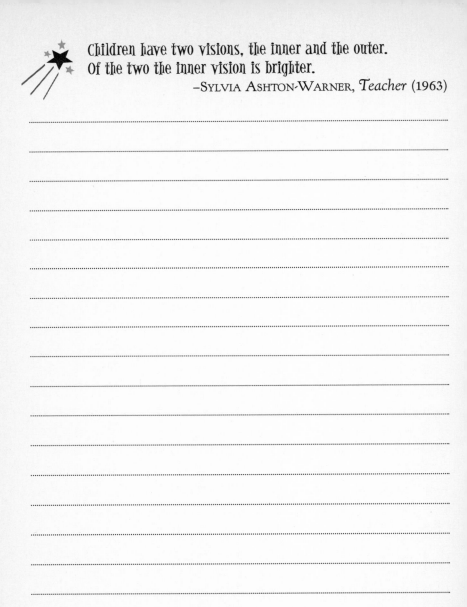

Children have two visions, the inner and the outer.
Of the two the inner vision is brighter.

–SYLVIA ASHTON-WARNER, *Teacher* (1963)

Don't worry. It doesn't help.

CANCER
June 21–July 20

Joe Souza was my second "husband." We were never legally married, but we lived together for eight years, and I had my youngest daughter Johanna with him. Joe was a Gloucester fisherman. He was also a heroin addict and a serious alcoholic who lived life as if it didn't matter if he died. Joe was safer out fishing than he was on shore, because in between trips he did nothing but get as high as he possibly could. With all of his problems, he was a real charmer, and I was crazy about him. Everyone knows that opposites attract, but why a spiritual space cadet like me hooked up with a charismatic drug fiend is a question I still can't answer. To this day I have no idea why that relationship even had to happen except for one thing: Johanna came out of it. Back in June 1985 Joe was fishing on the *Saint Lucia*. The boat came in before dawn on the day of the Summer Solstice, and he crawled into bed with me and the baby. He hung around at home until about suppertime, when he kissed us good-bye and said he was going downtown to look for a site. "Looking for a site" meant he was going to get high. By 10:30 that Midsummer Night, Joe's death wish finally came true. He went out like a comet and slipped through the veil on a fifth of expensive vodka and some dope that was stronger than usual.

Life and death are partners. They dance around us all the time. The solar force that gives everything life is so powerful at the

Summer Solstice it makes Midsummer Night one of *the* most magi-cal nights of the year. But wherever there is great light there is also great darkness, and the *moment* the Sun reaches its Zenith it starts to fade and begins a six-month-long Death March that culminates at the Winter Solstice. We are so blinded by what the light and heat have given life to that we lose sight of the fact that there's another side to it. The magic in the air on Midsummer Night is so electric you can feel it. And in that *instant,* when light and darkness become one, the marriage of the two creates a spark that gives rise to a spiritual force that is out of this world. Be mindful of what you wish for on this night: whatever you desire or have been dreaming about is ripe and ready to have all the strength of your focused intentions blown into it. Tonight is *the* night for all your best magic. If you're a witch, you know exactly what to do. If you're not a witch, don't worry. You can always throw a party to celebrate your dreams or go off by yourself and tune into them.

The Sun is moving through the sign Cancer for the next few weeks. Cancer's the sign of the Universal Mother, and thank God for her. We need all the maternal energy we can get right now, because this life and death dance has given birth to a new "child." The beauty pouring through each summer day is more than proof that your dreams are alive! They're blooming like flowers right here in front of you, and for the next month it's your job to nurse and water them with every ounce of tenderness you've got. The Sun may be dying, but you don't have time to grieve because you've got a little baby on your hands. If you're at a loss as to what to do, take your cue from Mother Nature. All she does in June and July is open up and allow her creations to blossom. Keep in mind that these may very well be your dreams, but they have a life of their own. This job is *way* bigger than it looks, because it's not just this cycle that you're "Mother" to. The seeds for every possible future vision are stored deep inside the ones you're nurturing now.

Joe Souza taught me more about life and death than anyone. It's perfect that he checked out on the night when underneath it all darkness had the upper hand. I spent eight years believing that if I just kept filling him with light and love he'd turn around. Little did I know that dark things have their place in the creation process too. Every time I look at Johanna I see all the beauty that came out of the dance we did. Her father's death gifted me with a deeper understanding of life and death and light and darkness. Whatever happens in the space between those polarities has something to do with God and love. When I was young I only wanted to see the light in everything. I had the notion that spiritual work would bring me to a point where everything would look beautiful and be perfect. What I've learned along the way is that the deeper you go with your spiritual work, the deeper the s__ gets! The good news is that the deeper the s___ gets, the more your light shines. It's simple and obvious, but it took me years to figure that out. I love the beauty and the warmth and the light that fills up the world when the Sun's in Cancer. I see it differently now that I know a little bit more about what the deal is here. Nothing in creation would be half so beautiful if there wasn't another side to it. So love the light, but remember that the darkness is what makes it shine.

It's all God, even the dark stuff.

There's no way around grief. You have no choice but to go through it, so feel your way and eventually you'll come out the other side.

It's easier to have someone die than it is to have them leave you. At least when they're dead you can't nurse the hope that that they'll come back or have to live with the fear that they might.

Wherever there is great light there is also great darkness.

In the face of all your suffering, never lose your openness and your willingness to remain vulnerable.

Love has no limits.

Love is the only thing that survives death.

....

....

....

....

....

....

....

....

....

....

....

....

....

....

Deal with your issues as best you can. If you don't handle them Mother Earth has to carry that weight for you and she's got enough on her mind.

Death is the ultimate disappearing act.

—KATE GREEN, *Night Angel* (1989)

I've been in love so many times and I still don't know anything about it.

The best way to give advice to your children is to find out what they want and tell them to go for it.

The higher you climb on the spiritual path the higher the mountain gets.

LEO
July 21–August 20

When I was a kid my parents took me to see the movie *Oklahoma*. I was only seven at the time, so I don't remember what it was about, but one thing stuck with me. My young imagination was overtaken by the vision Gordon MacRae created when he sang a song about the corn being as high as an elephant's eye and growing tall enough to reach the sky. For weeks afterward I wondered, "How high *is* an elephant's eye?" not believing it was possible for *anything* to grow that tall. I never knew what those words meant till I moved to Vermont. Up here corn is a big deal because they use it to feed the cows. If you drive through the fields in late July and all through August, the acres of corn look like regiments of huge Centurions. The corn grows *so tall* you get the feeling that if it got any bigger every row would come to life, start marching, and take over the whole planet!

Life gets so big it outdoes itself when the sun's in Leo. If Cancer's the Universal Mother, Leo is Mae West. Whenever I think of this sign I picture a ballsy, voluptuous female busting at the seams, strutting her stuff all over the place. There's something absolutely glorious about this time of year. Because the life force has completed whatever it was its intention to create, and all it wants to do is say, "Hey, look at me! Look at what I did! Aren't I awesome!"

Everything in creation needs love and praise, and it's time to give our dreams a standing ovation. We need to do this because it fuels our confidence that we *deserve* to have whatever we've been dreaming about. What's the point of doing all this work if we can't rejoice and revel in it? Because most of us have been trained to *not* fall too much in love with who we are and what we do, the business of appreciating our creations is stymied by the fact that we think we're being vain or egotistical if we do. The philosopher Georges Gurdjieff once said, "Self love is humanity's greatest problem when it is vanity, but you can't get enlightened without it." At a certain stage in any process, self-love and a radical sense of self-worth have to be developed. So forget about hiding your light under a bushel this month. When the Sun's in Leo it's totally appropriate to look in the mirror or anywhere else and say, "God, you're beautiful!" Because the truth is that you are, and so is everything you do.

In pre-Christian times the yearly gathering of the clans would happen somewhere between the last week of July and the first week of August. The Nordic people referred to this event as the *Althing*. The Celts and the Wiccans have always called it *Lughnassah* or *Lammas*. All the tribes would travel down from the highlands to a chosen place, and for a week or more everyone gathered to take care of business and whoop it up. These people went for months with little or no contact with the outside world; they had to practically kill themselves just to survive. As hard as they lived, they understood the importance of joyous celebration, and by the time the Althing came around they knew that, by God, they deserved to let it all hang out. Whenever there was any type of communal gathering, these people did it up in style, but Lammas was a total blast.

We have strayed so far from the Old Ways, and our connection to Nature just isn't there any more. The only thing we do that remotely resembles these early traditions is go to the county fair. And we're all so numbed by what being civilized has done to us we go to these things without feeling any connection to what they signify. The next time you take a trip to the county fair, check out the faces of the people there. They're there to entertain the kids maybe, but the fact that life is incredible has ceased to be an issue. The Pagans *knew* what they were celebrating. Their spiritual life was so closely linked to the rhythmic patterns of Nature they knew that they had come to honor the awesome power of the Great Mother in all her glory. They dressed up in scarlet and dragged out all their best finery just to reflect that glory. The men wore their gold helmets and carried their finest weapons. The women went over the top with their best duds too. *Everything* they had created or given life to came with them to the Althing. Their kids, their wares, their horses and livestock, all of it came along for the ride. And they displayed it with pride and laid it *all* out as an act of praise, not just for themselves but for the fact that *life* had done something absolutely incredible one more time again.

It's so important to honor ourselves, to honor life and what we do. And it's totally OK to be proud of who you are and what you have created. Like I said earlier, forget about hiding your light under a bushel while the Sun's in Leo. Go put on your best red dress, strap on some three-inch heels, put on all your best jewelry, and go dancing with the handsomest Viking you can find. For the next few weeks, celebrate and be joyful about the fact that life is glorious and so are you.

If you knew who you really are, you'd be amazed at your own magnificence.

Being in a joyful state is the key to everything.

Who said you had to be perfect? You **are** perfect!

There are no islands anymore.

–EDNA ST. VINCENT MILLAY (1940)

You are not separate. You are one with everything.

Accept **all** of who you are. Even the things you don't like about yourself are worthy of love. When you embrace it all, what you criticize becomes so infused with light and love it transforms naturally into your most precious gift.

Talk less. Listen more. You might learn something.

If you can't dress for success, at least dress for trying.

–LYNNE ALPERN AND ESTHER BLUMENFELD,
Oh, Lord, I Sound Just Like Mama (1986)

The world will come together in peace the day we realize that we share a common fate. If all of us don't thrive, none of us will.

Before you dump on anyone, remember, they're a mirror.

What's customary changes over time. Wearing lipstick once invited a death sentence. Now none of us would be caught dead without it!

The world never puts a price higher on you than the one you put on yourself.

–SONJA HENIE, *Wings on My Feet* (1940)

VIRGO
August 21–September 20

Y ou can't party all the time. Too much of a good thing is bad. And the celebratory energy that permeated the Unified Field while the Sun was in Leo has served its purpose. As soon as the Sun enters Virgo, the proverbial coach turns back into a pumpkin, and we have to face reality. If you just keep applauding yourself for being such a "beautiful dreamer," nine months of effort will go down the tubes. Even fruit rots on the vine if you don't pick it and find a way to preserve it. And while a good roll in the hay is undoubtedly fun, at some point we have to pull up our drawers, bale up the hay, and bring it into the barn or we'll be in big trouble come winter.

Harvesting our dreams is about getting down to business and doing something with them. The question is "What?" For the next few weeks we have to find a way to integrate them into our lives. In order to serve our highest good, everything we've done has to be assimilated and stored within us because it is part of our expe-rience now; it's part of who we are. When the visions from this cycle find their ultimate use, they will serve to nourish the visions of the next cycle; life is a continuous spiral and one dream begets another. And even though last year's dreams have fully materialized, they won't feed us indefinitely any more than one corn harvest will feed a herd of cows forever. So how do we place the lessons that have emerged from this cycle, and what do we know about life and ourselves that we didn't know before? Whatever we've learned is there to take us to the *next* level. Just like the schoolkids who move from one grade to another in early September, we're here to figure out how well last year's lessons have prepared us for what we don't know yet.

I have to confess, I am a Virgo. Most Virgos hate to admit it because all the astrology books have given us such a bad rap. They paint us up to be uptight, anal, nitpicking control freaks who do nothing but clean behind the refrigerator and work all the time. It's also widely accepted that all of us are prudes and none of us likes to get laid. No wonder we're self-conscious about telling people what sign we are! Who would want to be this way? It's taken me years to figure out what Virgos are really all about, and in the course of developing more love for myself I've developed a deep appreciation for this archetype.

Virgo is the point in the Zodiac where the real world and the world of Spirit become one. It's where the Hermetic axiom, "As above, so below," installs itself in the collective mind. The obsessive-compulsive tendencies that are characteristic of most Virgos spring from a deep desire to witness spiritual perfection or see it reflected on the physical plane. The need for order, the love of purity, and the willingness to work harder than anyone else come out of an innate understanding that behind what is apparent, absolutely everything we do is really a sacred act. When the Sun's in Virgo what is of this Earth is being consecrated and blessed so that it can symbolically be handed over to its ultimate purpose. The fruit that gets picked off the vine doesn't become truly glorious until it goes through the alchemical process that preserves it for future use. Transmuting lead into gold is sacred work. And at this point in the dream cycle, our visions are being transmuted so that we can bring them into the core of our being and understand at a deeper level how they are meant to serve us.

Virgo is the sign of the High Priestess. In the Egyptian temples, the High Priestesses were the intermediaries who superintended the rituals that kept life going in the right direction. They knew where all the sacred objects needed to be placed so that the proper energies got stirred. They were also the guardians of the sexual mysteries and acted as conduits for the spiritual force that comes through all of us at the sexual level. Contrary to popular opinion, the Vestal Virgins were far from celibate. It was part of *their job* or their ultimate purpose to be sexual. It's hilarious to me that Virgos are written off as prudish. I think it has something to do with the fact that the sexual force and the spiritual force were so intermingled in the Priestess archetype. And 13,000 years of patriarchal programming have led us to believe that sex and God can't occupy the same space, so Virgo can only be seen in public as the Resident Prude! The truth is that all the power and force of creation resides within the womb of the female. It's no mystery. The sacred and the profane are one and the same.

God and light flow through absolutely everything. The fine line between what is apparent and the spiritual energy that fuels it may be invisible, but it's the point where we can tap into our own divinity. There's so much more to what we do than meets the eye. All the visions that we've fostered have spent nine months in the womb of creation. And they are on the verge of being alchemically transmuted so that their highest purpose can be served. Open your heart to that idea, and use this month to recognize that all of life and everything you do is sacred.

Everything is light.

Look into the eyes of everyone you meet and see God reflected there.

I always thought that Spirit was the prime mover. But the fact that it "moved across the waters of the deep" implies that the Great Void was here first. The Female Principle has to be where all of this came from.

There are many, many gates to the sacred and they are
wide as we need them to be.

—SHERRY RUTH ANDERSON AND PATRICIA HOPKINS,
The Feminine Face of God (1991)

Every crisis is an opportunity to break out of the patterns that keep you stuck.

To really move along the spiritual path you have to be
totally willing to surrender every single one of your most
cherished illusions.

May all the divergent energies on this planet reblend into harmony, and may we come to recognize what is sacred in our lives.

–DRUNVALO MELCHIZEDEK

....

....

....

....

....

....

....

....

....

....

....

....

....

....

....

....

....

 Everyone is a beam of pure, white light traveling
at a frequency that's slow enough for them to take
on a human form.

We are not human beings learning to be spiritual;
we are spiritual beings learning to be human.

—JACQUELINE SMALL, *Awakening in Time* (1991)

Integrity has to do with living your truth even
when it's inconvenient, costly, or life threatening.

Being involved in spiritual things doesn't automatically make you spiritual.

If you can keep your cool when everyone around you is losing theirs and blaming you for it, you'll probably be able to walk on water too!

LIBRA
September 21–October 20

N ow that our visions have found their place, it's time to see what happens when they start to mingle with all the other dreams that are floating around out there. "No man is an island," and eventually something *else* has to become part of every equation. It's so perfect that as soon as this "other" becomes the primary issue, the Sun starts spinning through what's commonly under-stood as "the relationship" sign. We're also at the halfway mark in the circle of constellations, and Libra is where we find out who we are relative not just to our "other half," but to *everything* that's out there. I have a lot of judgments about this sign that come from God knows where. I have always pooh-poohed Libra as way too super-ficial and boring. It's anything but. From a cosmic perspective, this is the horizon line where Earth and Sky connect, and what hap-pens at this interface is absolutely awesome.

I have a feeling it's time to talk about relationships. I've been through the mill with them, and I'm sure you have too. Most of us were fed the notion that you fall in love with someone and it lasts forever. I don't know about you, but it didn't work that way for me. And my failed attempts to match those pictures of perfection brought me to the conclusion that it would make more sense if I went out and got a different frame for them. Ever since I've loos-ened up about what it's possible to do in this area of my life, I've realized that relationships are way bigger than we allow them to be. But whether we choose to take the "normal" route or prefer to color outside the lines, one thing is true for all of us: The most important relationship we have is the one we have with ourselves.

Every person we connect with is a reflection of what's going on inside us. And the internal marriage between our male and our female aspect has to be fully balanced before we can do anything constructive with another person. This is easier said than done, and the work required to maintain the inner connection never stops. And even if you maintain it, there's no guarantee that any of your relationships will remain permanent, because all of us grow and change. And if your growth rate exceeds your partner's or takes you off in a new direction, the reflection in the mirror will bear no resemblance to who you've become. It *may* be possible for two people to grow as individuals and move upward and onward at the same rate of motion. I have never experienced this but I don't discount it. But ultimately all our relationships are temporary because people die. This may be a hard pill to swallow, but it's the truth. The only permanent relationship is the one you have with yourself.

So where does this deep longing to be connected to "other" in a meaningful way came from? I think it comes from the need we all have to be recognized for who we really are. When someone loves you, they love who you are. And their love for you helps you to see everything about what that is and inspires you to be *more* of who you are. Ultimately that love awakens us to the God within. The need for "other" and the burning desire to see ourselves reflected in the eyes of another person come from a yearning to experience our own divinity and be reminded that we are loved unconditionally by whatever is at the source.

By the Fall Equinox, whatever we've been dreaming about along with everyone else's visions have reached their highest mode of expression. And none of us can grow any further if we don't figure out how to weave what we've created into the universal matrix. What's out there is dying to embrace us the same way

Father Sky embraces Mother Earth at the horizon. In order for that to happen, we have to surrender all of who we are and all of what we've become as a result of this dream process to something outside of ourselves. What good would it do to keep it all inside? How would it benefit anyone if we didn't take our show on the road and see where we fit in to the greater whole? The horizon line is the point where every vision falls in love with its larger purpose. And we can only find out what that is by sharing what's inside us with the world.

There are a million ways to do this. All of us exist in relation to *everything,* so the possibilities and the points through which we can connect are infinite. When we open up our hearts to the people and experiences that are out there wanting to share what they have to give us, something magical happens. We get to see that we are not separate from *anything* and that God flows through it *all.* What we are part of is much greater than we realize, and the whole point of being here in 3D is to remember our own divinity. If all of us understood this, life on planet Earth would be so different, because we would know that we are all one and that we come from the same source.

Use this month to find out as much as you can about where you connect with what's out there. Relinquish your separateness. Let the God in you come through. When you do you will see it reflected in the eyes of everyone you meet and in everything you do.

....

....

....

....

....

....

....

....

....

....

....

....

....

....

....

....

....

 When I was young I got lost in my relationships. Now that I'm old I find myself in them.

Every single one of your relationships is as rewarding as the one you have with your significant other. You can go deep and far with everyone.

The loneliest woman in the world is a woman without a
close woman friend.

–Toni Morrison

My friends are my most valuable resources.

If you're lying to yourself, it's impossible to be truthful with anyone else.

Jealousy is the illusion that there's not enough love to go around.

You can't **make** anyone happy. They have to be happy.

We're all on our way back to the source.

Lord, let me be an instrument of thy peace.

—SAINT FRANCIS

Your kids don't listen to you because they have to make their own mistakes.

As hard as it may be to accept, everyone is lovable.

What's keeping you in your relationship?

SCORPIO
October 21–November 20

The Sun's entrance into Scorpio is hard to miss if you've got your eyes peeled. The trees stand naked against the bare landscape, the sky turns gray, the atmosphere gets raw, and all of a sudden the Earth that was once beautiful and alive feels like a gothic cemetery. The 21st of October marks the beginning of what was once known as "The Meat Harvest." If it sounds bloodthirsty and cruel it very well may be, but life has a million different faces. And while many of us nowadays consider it "déclassé" to hunt, back in the old times it wasn't something people intellectualized about. It was a necessity.

What fascinates me about this part of the yearly cycle is that the minute we leave the sweetness and light of the Libran frequency we get sucker-punched by something dark and ruthless. As soon as the Sun enters Scorpio, death and dying are the name of the game. How in God's name do we go from love to death? What's the explanation for this harsh transition? The truth is, love and death are intimately entwined. Anyone who's ever really been in love knows what I'm talking about. In the deepest moments of lovemaking each individual has to surrender his or her own separateness in order to experience orgasm. The Victorians referred to orgasm as "The Little Death." They may have been prudes, but they were obviously onto something. You don't even know where you stop and the other person begins in that moment, because something in you has to die to feel love.

The most important Pagan cross-quarter happens this month. The cosmic portal is wide open on October 31, and Halloween or Samhain is the Wiccan New Year. The Christians knew all about what this passage meant to the Pagans. They turned Halloween into a joke, but they invented All Saints' Day or The Day of the Dead and slipped it in on November 1 so that the converts would feel at home with the "New Religion."

The Wiccan take on October 31 is that it's a time to bury the past in preparation for the future. Halloween is a ritual that honors the passing of all the dreams we have created and a celebration of the new life that will spring forth from them in the next cycle. From a mythological perspective, October 31 is the point where Ceres parts ways with her daughter Persephone and sends her down into the Underworld to live with Hades, her father. What we're supposed to do between Samhain and the Winter Solstice is travel deep into our own underworld and acquaint ourselves with all the issues that stand between us and the full development of the dreams that we will birth in the coming year. Nature's light is steadily decreasing now, and the darkness that shrouds us is a sign that we can only go within to find a different kind of light.

I've heard it said that the only way you can really begin to see is in total darkness. And that may be true, because it's the issues of our Shadow Self that keep us from being fully who we are. And if we don't use this time to look them over one last time and close the casket on whatever they represent, we won't evolve. By the time the Sun returns on the Winter Solstice, we should have enough clarity about what lies beneath to move forward unencumbered by it.

The real meaning and the beauty behind all of the Halloween traditions has been lost. We dress up in ghoulish costumes, we carve up pumpkins and light them with candles, and we put the focus on all kinds of sinister stuff, but we're oblivious to why. In the Old Times the reason everyone wore Halloween costumes was so that on New Year's night they could *be* the image of what they saw themselves *becoming* in the next cycle. It was a magical way to imprint what they wanted for themselves in the universal matrix. Hollowed-out pumpkins were symbols for the womb of the Great Mother. And the candles placed inside them were a sign to all that the light at this time of year shines only within. The skeletons and the emphasis on "creepy" things are about owning our greatest fears.

The dark stuff has its place and is just as rich and valuable as the sweetness and light. The real beauty of this cross-quarter and the season it holds sway over is that this is where the darker forces meet and become one with whatever we *do* want to acknowledge. And when you erase the line that separates good and bad, fear and love, and life and death, you see that it's all just God here. The deeper reasons why the Pagans honored Halloween are shrouded by whatever has caused us to forget. But somewhere inside we know what the truth is, because it's more powerful than the forces that have kept it hidden.

Don't expect to be on top of things right now. Explore the passageways that you've closed yourself off to and make every effort to see what's in them. Think about what you don't want to see, and ask yourself why it scares you so much. Bring it all into the light and embrace it. When you do, you'll discover that absolutely everything about you is Godlike.

Pain and suffering nudge you, one way or another, toward growth and healing.

Every answer lies within. All we have to do is listen to our hearts.

Your worst fears are nothing compared to what would happen if you didn't face them.

Using the past to predict the future is never a wise idea.

You cannot find peace by avoiding life.

The human heart is remarkable. The more it breaks,
the more it can hold and the stronger it gets.

There is no separation between the inner and outer worlds. Whatever you're experiencing, be it bad or good, is a reflection of your inner state.

The heart within is where God resides.

Everything you do is OK. Even if you chain smoke and eat red meat, you can still reach God. It's all the same to Him.

Don't live in the past. It's over. Be here in the moment because the future is **now**.

Your lessons here never end.

I am grateful for everything that has happened to me.

SAGITTARIUS
November 21–December 20

T hank God whoever invented the Zodiac slipped Sagittarius in right after Scorpio. Scorpio energy is *so* intense, and "Sag" is much more happy-go-lucky. Even though we're not out of the woods as far as the darkness goes, by the 21st of November we have a totally different perspective on it. Jupiter, the planet of optimism, joy, and abundance, rules Sagittarius. The nice thing about this sign is that it's loaded with faith that everything's going to be all right no matter how awful life gets. Knowing that everything is in divine order makes it a hell of a lot easier to be human, and the idea that God's out there watching over all of us is what the Sagittarian archetype brings to the astrological party.

The holiday season kicks off around this time. Thanksgiving gets the ball rolling, and we gather together with those we love to feast and give thanks for what we have. As soon as we've cleared the table, our minds are on Hanukkah and Christmas. And everyone goes out and starts spending all kinds of money buying stuff to give away. We light up our houses, and the gene that makes people want to bake starts working overtime. There are parties everywhere, and we spend the next few weeks going off the deep end eating and drinking.

My family's all Swedish, and when I was a kid my Auntie Greta would put on this unbelievable holiday smorgasbord. I was a chubby little girl, and this event was like having a free pass to heaven. My Auntie Annie was always there. It was the only time I ever got to see her. Auntie Annie wore way too much costume jewelry, and when she had enough Glug she'd go on and on about her "darling Freddie" and her life as a burlesque queen. Auntie Greta was into gaudy, shiny decorations, and everything in the house was lit up and covered with tinsel.

There were presents for everyone. I remember one year Auntie Greta gave me three pairs of tights with shiny threads in them. She got them at The Bargain Center, which was the 1950s equivalent of The Dollar Store, and those sparkly tights made me the most popular girl in the third grade. It wasn't till I got older that I found out that Auntie Greta's life sucked! I'm pretty sure Auntie Annie's life was no picnic either. God knows what those women had to live through, but they sure didn't let it interfere with their Christmas spirit.

What *is* it about this time of year that makes us put all the bad stuff on the back burner and focus on what's good about life? For four weeks our hearts overflow with a spirit of abundance and generosity that includes even those who have nothing. Back when I was *really* poor, standing in line at the local food shelf was like hitting the jackpot during the holidays. As humiliating as it was to be on the dole, I was eternally grateful to all the benevolent souls who were kind enough to share what they had with me and my kids. One year I got a two-pound bag of hazelnut coffee at the food cupboard, and it blew me away. From the time I was six years old my Swedish Aunties would say, "Come on Carolyn, sit with us and have your coffee like a good Swede." Coffee is my favorite treat. and at that moment I was so broke this gift was proof to me that there *is* a God.

Something in our hearts knows without a doubt that we are cradled in the arms of God or some higher power that is always there, protecting us from whatever it is that's causing us fear. It's called Faith. The illusion of safety that money, power, position, and even education provide exempts none of us from poverty of the spirit. If you don't have Faith you have nothing. It's the most valuable commodity in the world.

The truth about life is that in every moment we are swimming in a sea of love, joy, and abundance. It's easy to lose sight of this, because our experiences often create the illusion that exactly the opposite is true. In those times when we are suffering the most, we forget all about the truth. We curse God and blame life for victimizing us until we realize that it gets us nowhere. Then something in us lets go. And we become open to the idea that, regardless of what is going on, it's all exactly as it should be whether we comprehend it or not. Faith has to do with trusting that even the bad stuff is good and that someday we will know what purpose it served.

When we look back on our troubles from a distance, we often see how much they contributed to our growth and understanding. I have finally realized that the rough stuff is a greater gift than the stuff that's a piece of cake. And the nice thing about this time of year is that we collectively acknowledge that it's all good. From a cosmic perspective, we are still in the heart of darkness while the sun's in Sagittarius. But there's light at the end of the tunnel, and the belief that it's there is reinforced by the fact that every year since the dawn of time the Sun comes back on the Winter Solstice. It always has and it always will.

The heart of God within you is the place where Faith resides. Use this month to find your way there. The new visions that will come alive in a few weeks need a space that's big enough to hold them. So, open up. Let all the joy and love you feel go out into the world, and remember to keep the Faith.

Faith is that quality of power by which the things desired become the things possessed.

          –Kathryn Kuhlman, I Believe in Miracles (1962)

You are the source of your abundance.

Everything is the opposite of what it appears to be.

No human problem can be solved by thinking, since thinking itself is the problem. The end of knowledge is the beginning of wisdom.

—KRISHNAMURTI

Don't worry too much about what anyone has to say about what you do or don't do. They don't have to live your life.

They say that if you get bored enough with calamity
you will learn to laugh.

–Lawrence Durrell

Be patient with all the unsolved questions in your heart.
Time and experience will answer them.

Everything is going to be all right.

If it ain't broke, don't fix it.

–Anonymous

Always smile at the cashier and ask them how they're doing. Being a cashier is one of the most demanding jobs on the planet.

There are no mistakes.

I know
The soft wind will blow me home.

—Yü Hsüan-chi (9th century)